LEARNING FROM LONGHOUSE

JACK LENOR LARSEN

POINTED LEAF PRESS

CONTENTS

8   *"I have a grounding primarily in design, and some in architecture, with experience in materials and colors, as well as a keen interest in structure and texture."*

14   *"On schooldays I dreamed what I would build on the weekend."*

16   *"The space was informal, relaxed, flexible, and exquisite."*

32   *"LongHouse is a Case Study in an alternative lifestyle."*

36   *"Ise Shrine remains the most remarkable structure for its power and nuance."*

38   *"Set back 1,000 feet from the road, LongHouse has a succession of approaches."*

52   *"I wanted the house to be not just functional but concerned with the senses of delight, of freedom, of being secure—open and happy."*

72   *"Buying plants small and early is key."*

88   *"Sculpture in the garden forms strong focal points, sometimes anchoring vistas."*

110   *"Building collections of any size or material is the surest means to affirming our identity."*

PREVIOUS PAGES LEFT The Polish-American architect Daniel Libeskind's *Spirit House Chair*, a custom-made limited edition design, to coincide with the opening of the new Michael Crystal building at the Royal Ontario Museum, in Ontario, Canada. OPPOSITE The site-specific outdoor version of multimedia artist Yoko Ono's *Play It By Trust* is one of the centerpieces of the gardens at LongHouse. Built in 1999, the conceptual work consists of a white cement and marble-dust 16 x 16-foot board and 32 large pieces. Ono is the first artist to transform the concept of chess, changing it from a game of aggression to one of peace, and making it a metaphor for hope.

FROM WEAVER TO GARDENER

In the second half of the 20th century, I was known as the textile designer who was dedicated to architecture. My forte was the structure, the materials, and the process of craft methods in the Third World. I also designed dinnerware, carpets, and fabrics for airlines, but the most successful of these products were terry cloth towels and Wilton carpets usually created by graphic designers. But as a weaver, I could still work within the full potential of the craft process. The yards of hand-spun, ungraded fibers were my favorites in a dozen countries; the resist patterning technique through textiles such as batik and ikat was also a favorite. I had become a key player in the Craft movement, a curator, and an author of influential museum exhibitions and books. And although I gardened as a boy, I still today remain beholden to all those who know more about gardens and gardening. While I admit to not being a "plantsman," and am ignorant of Latin, my decades of gardening have imbued in me some understanding of the needs of common plants. So, what do I really have? I believe it is a grounding primarily in design, and some in architecture, with experience in materials and colors as well as a keen interest in structure and texture. The fact that I worked in numerous countries opened alternatives to conventional ways of thinking. Thirty-nine trips to Japan sharpened my passion for understatement. A citizen of the world since my school days, I veered away from the commonplace. As a child of the Great Depression, I am still deeply concerned with "making do," with seeking

alternatives, and with subsidizing one cost with another's savings. During my first decades in New York, when I usually worked weekends and traveled only for business, I read the French author André Gide. Although a prolific writer, he always seemed to be gardening. I always wondered how this was possible. For 30 years, my firm and I were constantly moving, expanding, and improving either our showroom, offices, and studio—or my rented apartments. Although we often employed architects, I was the space planner and display director. Floor plans became my specialty. But all these were temporary solutions for rented spaces. Building permanent houses with personal funds would be quite different. There have been three such residences, but from each experience, I was better able to conceive the next one.
—JACK LENOR LARSEN

OPPOSITE Jack Lenor Larsen was photographed by the New York photographer Roberto Dutesco.

OVERLEAF East Hampton-based photographer Dell R. Cullum used a drone for this image of the *Red Garden*.

PREVIOUS PAGES American sculptor Judith Shea's 2011–2012 *Idol*, in cast bronze, stainless steel, and aluminum, has been placed in the sunken garden near the house. ABOVE Jack Lenor Larsen gazes toward a fog-bound garden from a dining room window. The iconic table and chairs are from Wharton Esherick's historic exhibition at the 1939 World's Fair.

"There should be as many types of houses as there are people living."
—FRANK LLOYD WRIGHT

The story of LongHouse began long ago when, at the age of three, I collected seedling trees to make my own garden and, when I was four, made my first shelters. At five, I led playmates on forays—sometimes into swamps, nettles—and even mutiny! This only child was a nonconforming loner, an explorer, and a maker. I built boats but sold, not sailed, them. **On school days, I imagined what we would build on the weekend.** It was almost always a place not to be in, but one to build together. Perhaps because my dad was a builder of houses, I have always been aware of architecture and interior space. Our Depression-era Sundays were often spent touring model houses. Studying architecture, particularly interior architecture, was a dream. I enjoyed the structural aspects, preferring building models to drawing—and found myself a better builder than painter. Finally, I switched courses to become a weaver—building fabrics out of real materials so they would be durable. Like architecture, these textiles' horizontal and vertical structures were dependent on materials with highlight and shadow. In six years of college, I outfitted a series of rooms to live in, and so, too, the studios and apartments that followed. Still, all of these places were rented, not owned, and therefore not permanent. From the Japanese loft onwards, this would change. Decisions were no longer stage sets but deeper, durable, and *mine*. —J.L.L.

THE JAPANESE LOFT

Early on, I had been fortunate to find a 19th century top-floor loft near our design studio in Greenwich Village, with a ceiling of arched tiles punctuated with skylights, and a view from the terrace of the Statue of Liberty! As I was leaving for Asia on a business trip, I left a bid on it. Arriving in Beijing, China, a friend of mine, Philip Cutler, replied, "That sounds so right— use my cablegram to raise your bid $10,000." The response came back quickly, "You went up $15,000, but it's yours! Attached is a small floor plan." While working in Japan, I sat on the floor of the ryokan in which I was staying to lay it out. As the Japanese don't have dining rooms or bedrooms, I decided that I would not, either. Soon, I was back in New York just long enough to hand my floor plan to Charles Forberg, my architect. I had then sent him a telex to say "I want a sense of the structure and materials." Slowly, the best Japanese builder we could find achieved this goal. Eventually, 50 fabric-covered sliding doors lined the long sidewalls of the loft. They would conceal the existing jumble of the walls while providing generous shelving. As the north and south window walls were above a 30-inch–high sill, I raised the floors with a deck accommodating a hot tub and a series of storage bins that could be rolled out as extra seating. White floor tiles multiplied daylight from skylights above. The space—as pleasurable when I was alone as when filled with guests—was informal, relaxed, flexible, and exquisite. My friends called the loft "Square House."

OPPOSITE While the loft was minimalistic, it was not without sybaritic comforts: A black soaking tub doubled as a reflecting pool; the bed was covered in quilted silk; and a custom-made fireplace was installed.

LEFT For a late evening buffet supper at the loft, the south room is all aglow. The sofas have been stowed under the deck, and storage boxes with seat pads rolled out along the right wall. Guests gathered for cocktails in the north room, then led into this space.

ROUND HOUSE

For my first thirty years in New York, my firm and I were both constantly moving, expanding and improving, either the showroom, offices, studio or my rented apartments. Although we often employed architects, I was the space planner and display director.

By the end of the 1950s, the Modernism I felt part of seemed reduced to a style of boxy white rooms with glass walls and rather expected furnishings. When the concept of the hand-built personal house became my attractive alternative, I recalled seeing—when I was nine years old—an early documentary of the young Princess Elizabeth touring the British Western African colonies. I remember being captivated by the houses that were ingeniously crafted from every kind of material. I vowed at the time, "One day I shall see them!" So, in 1960 I went to Nigeria, where these houses were even better than I remembered. A man's three wives each had a round house, and the sons in the family had small ones. Together, these structures created both sunny and shade-filled outdoor living spaces. In South Africa, I saw houses with small rooms wrapped halfway around a central room— multiple outer rooms that could accommodate rectangular beds and such without creating pie shapes within the circle. The houses were far more compelling than the ones we had at home. In East Hampton, New York, in the early 1960s, I built a house made up of three round structures

OPPOSITE An aerial view shows the layout of three of the buildings at Round House, the compound built in 1964, and inspired by the Bantu culture of West Africa.

plus a series of circular gardens and a swimming pool. By 1965, Round House had become the most published house in America. It was personal, unique, and as handcrafted as possible. The American ceramicist, Karen Karnes, crafted the handmade stoneware fireplaces, plumbing fixtures, and half-ton finials that topped the conical roofs. The clerestory stained-glass windows seemed to be at one with the gardens outside. When the dense concrete walls—my protest against glass houses—proved too confining, I added a glass-roofed conservatory to the south. The separate structures allowed for guests to be happy in their own spaces, and I was delighted with my detached studio.

RIGHT The guest house is one of three structures at Round House that was inspired by West African rondavels.

OPPOSITE The new dining room in the main house faces west, toward a wide plaza divided by the rill leading to the Bill Moss pavilion.

RIGHT Built as a studio from the wooden forms of the main house's concrete walls, the Silk House derives its name from the handwoven tussah silk on the walls and ceiling—affordable because the silk was a "mistake" and unsale-able. The fireplace is the exposed insert from a Heatilator, providing maximum warmth at little cost. The wooden chairs are African. The basketry chairs are by the Danish designer Nanna Ditzel for Larsen Furniture.

For years I had been clearing the expansive, bland acreage adjacent to Round House, editing the thousands of trees and monster vines, taming it with a maze of grass paths, and clearing an open meadow. Evergreens were added to lighten the winter-grey oaks. I had already created the *Red Posts* and the amphitheater in an indifferent forest. Next to Round House were 16 acres of affordable woodlands I had purchased for protection. The most likely setting for the house was the worst tangle of broken trees and monster vines now circled by grassy paths and new hemlock hedges that defined where, in the 18th century, field boundaries had been built with earth. A woodsman cleared the land in exchange for firewood. Positioning a house that was not yet designed required some imagination. Before clearing the plot, my friend Peter Olsen and I had climbed a tall ladder to experience the view and feel what the breezes could be on a main floor that would be ten feet off the ground...as the most iconic aspect of the Ise Grand Shrine in Mie, Japan, is its massive gables, we made 37-foot-high "gables" with

LEFT AND OVERLEAF On acquiring the acres for LongHouse, we found a score of cedar logs killed by the deep shade of new oaks. As the logs were durable but in all sizes, the thought for this Study in Heightened Perspective came to mind. The two rows of posts were spaced ever closer, smaller, and shorter. I chose the red paint because the red Torii gates in Japan are so striking against foliage. We then added red azaleas—cheap and quite unexciting-looking until massed. The large, hand-built vessel at the end is by the famous Japanese potter, Toshiko Takaezu. Red-leaved Japanese maples and plum trees complete the setting. In winter, when the eerie silence tends to dramatize the sightlines, the composition is breathtaking. I made this composition 40 years ago, and still wonder why no project since is as perfect or as much photographed.

bamboo! And it seemed that the sale of the ten acres of Round House would be able to finance a larger house. (It didn't.) Then came some setbacks. Round House finally sold for half the estimate we had thought it would. And as we were cutting down the massive oak trees, I imagined their sturdy trunks as the pillars supporting the house. Jokan, the Japanese builder who was advising us, said that oak wood never stops expanding and contracting. When he wanted nine Japanese roofers for a year, we gave up on Jokan, along with a wooden structure. Charles Forberg and I would go on alone building the house in masonry—stucco over cement, with floor tiles and roofing tiles. Their low maintenance and fire resistance proved a plus. This would be my 30th collaboration with Charles, who had finally come around to my way of thinking as a craftsmaker, making decisions as work progressed. Off we went on what Charles said was to be a "fast track"— that lasted for five years!

RIGHT The Napa Valley, California-based Molly Chappellet photographed this aerial view of LongHouse showing the house and the pond in mid-September.

During the Post-World War II years in Southern California, about two dozen Case Study Houses were built—mostly by younger architects—to demonstrate settings for a new, informal Modern lifestyle. Modest in cost and size for families without staff, they were meant to function as meaningful new modes of living. The publication and visitation of these pacesetting houses sped up the spread of Modernism—from the West Coast eastward, then internationally. The time was right. After many years of the Depression and war, we were all ready to change to a new way of living for a younger audience in a booming economy.

But what had started as a revolution became stereotyped and predictable, and evolved into a rather conformist style, soon to be displaced, as many designers focused on larger, more trade-oriented buildings. Still, the concept of a fully dimensional, living Case Study, one that can be shared and visited, seems a useful one. LongHouse is a Case Study in an alternative lifestyle. When the house is no longer a residence, it will be available to visitors. Then the whole house will be a museum full of broad collections of modern furnishings that we can all learn from—and that can buoy our own individuality.

While I was still at Round House, my African compound next door, I was considering the genesis of sharing. Friends who visited would suggest, "as you spend all your time and means on this garden, why not share it with others?" I found myself soon discussing this possibility with the East Hampton Town Board. Its members treated me like Santa Claus—saying it would suit them wonderfully—with the maintenance underwritten, of course! I didn't jump with the giving of Round House, but later, when envisioning the more ambitious LongHouse project, sharing that property was always in my mind. Even with the brilliance of color photography, or even film, experiencing a space in person could be felt more deeply than looking at photographs. I envisioned LongHouse as a personal house in a dynamic, evolving garden—a demonstration of living "outside the box." LongHouse would be another example of resisting the common urge to conform as readily as sheep. And our improvising and making do with what was on hand would stimulate a broader creativity. The pond was scooped out by a giant bulldozer, excavating sufficient subsoil to build the massive dune by the house and to finish the protective berms along the road. (Achieving two goals with a single effort still delights me!)

LEFT As the lotus pond at Round House was so successful, we decided that the one at LongHouse would be larger and could be overseen from the house. The headless figure is one of a pair of *Rabdomante* or dowser aluminum sculptures—symbolizing a search for underground water—by Polish artist Magdalena Abakanowicz.

NAIKU MAIN SHRINE. 伊勢大廟内宮正殿

THE ISE GRAND SHRINE

Twenty-five years after building Round House, as I came back from a visit to Stanley Marcus' sprawling adobe, with its rooms dedicated to art but having no other function, I realized that *if* I were ever to start over, I, too, could have a house with "waste space." A book on the Ise Grand Shrine, in Ise, Mie, Japan, greeted my return home. Long my favorite architecture—on stilts, with massive roofs—Ise offered both a challenge and an alternative. The seventh century Ise Shinto shrine is "pre-Japanese" in a style believed to be Southeast Asian. It speaks of Japan before the influence of China and Buddhism. As the major Shinto edifice, Ise is where the emperor is crowned King of Heaven. Also unique is its being rebuilt every 20 years so craftsmen will remember the complex joinery of its wooden structure. To me, Ise remains the most remarkable structure for its power and nuance. From a base of coarse gravel, wooden columns raise these buildings off the ground, while massive roofs cap them magnificently. In all, Ise is quite extraordinary—and certainly the inspiration for LongHouse—more modest in size but still lofty and unconventional. Ise offered us a fresh take on "Modernism," with an opportunity to have a variety of spaces and ceiling heights. The structure was boldly expressed, as were the materials.

OPPOSITE A vintage postcard shows one of 125 buildings comprising the Ise Shrine compound in Mie, Japan.

When approaching too many American homes, one is first aware of only the front door. Too many driveways also lead straight in, revealing too much at the outset. The experience would be richer with even such a minor prologue as a gate or archway. So, at LongHouse, the driveway curves and rises—revealing nothing, but heightening one's expectations. Set back 1,000 feet from the road, LongHouse has a succession of approaches: First at roadside, then across the graveled parking lot, and then toward an entry garden to the GateHouse.

RIGHT Ray's Way, an allée of Cryptomeria Yoshino—originally planted in the late 1980s—offers a majestic entree into LongHouse.

RIGHT The necessarily long path from the parking lot to GateHouse is as welcoming as possible, with seasonal blossoms and a pair of white-leafed willows, the stems of which, in the fall, will turn a burnished crimson. The fact that the walk is wheelchair-accessible would be appropriate for any residence. The path functions as a prologue to the park-like spaces inside GateHouse.

LEFT The GateHouse welcomes visitors to the gardens beyond. The climbing White Dawn Rose was given by a rosarian, claiming it to be a "fine rose for a poor place." It is! Never watered, fed, or sprayed, we only occasionally cut off dead blossoms, but seldom prune. Bravo!

RIGHT Past the GateHouse, the path winds through a long arc of sand dunes to the stairs and the landscape beyond. American glass artist Dale Chihuly's *Cobalt Reeds* dates from 2000.

LEFT The gentle steps
of railroad ties and
garnet stone lead past
xeriscaping herbals,
up the berm toward
the front entrance.

Most aspects of making—whether an arrangement or a place setting, stay put. Gardens do
not. Plants may wither, expire, become crowded,
or simply grow! As a designer, I have for too
many years composed plantings in relation to
their present size, and then had to laboriously
move them to allow for growth. This is often
costly and destructive to surrounding areas, as
well as time consuming. Slowly I learned that
changes in a garden are to be celebrated.
The majesty of mature, well-pruned oaks in
winter brings tears to my eyes. While one of
the pleasures of the Japanese landscape is their
favoring of evergreens, this was not so on the
original LongHouse land. Monotonously flat, the
acres were darkened in summer by a dense
cover of second-growth oaks. In winter,
their bare grey trunks were so tedious that the
first plants we put in were 100 deeply discounted
rhododendron maximum. The gaudy color
of their blossoms has now been ameliorated by
the admixture of named varieties.

RIGHT Curved walks are favored at LongHouse.
Because of increased traffic, gravel of various colors
has replaced many of our grass paths. A symphony
of evergreen textures frames the house approached
by a Moon Bridge that supports wisteria. The soft
red of the garnet stone path is complementary to
the evergreens and, with nearly the same color value,
maintains the horizontal plane of the area.

OPPOSITE The Moon Bridge leads visitors from the garden to the second floor of the house. The approach to the bridge is covered by low-growing conifers, and by wisteria on the railings.

RIGHT To the left and south of the red doors that lead into the entrance conservatory, one can see the ground-level pavilion, and the overhung windows of the living room, with its large skylights.

The house wasn't to be "old" or "new," but personal and accommodating. I wanted it to be not just functional but concerned with the senses of delight, of freedom, of being secure—and therefore, open and happy. This concept parallels the long-sought fourth dimension of how we feel in a situation, how we emotionally respond to a space—whether it be a mountaintop or a shelter. Historically, home was once a property near a small town— where everything was familiar, where everything was "ours." Nowadays, whether we have the possibility of having multiple homes with numerous rooms or live in less space, we need to reconnect with that feeling of being comfortable at home. LongHouse would also be first and foremost a Case Study with the strength of Modernism, but demonstrating alternatives to convention. Its free-flowing garden spaces would feel more Japanese than American and—as in Japan—they would embrace the four seasons. Indoor spaces would express scale, structure, and a sense of materials. They would be practical, for low maintenance. (They still are!) The tile floors are impervious to gardeners' boots and the fireproof tiled roof will be there for 200 years. The small elevator is a godsend, and so are the massive, accommodating basements. Having the main floor on the second level encourages cool breezes as well as improved vistas. That the windows are protected from the sun by massive eaves serves us well, as does the 65-foot-long skylight at the roof's apex and a glass-ceilinged conservancy—with tinted double glazing, impervious to heat and insulated against the cold, which guarantees solar warming while providing lovely light for plants as well as people! The daylight is so pleasant in these spaces that they have become our favorite rooms, where we live when we can't be on the veranda. We also outfitted LongHouse with an industrial furnace with seven independent heating zones, any of which can be turned off when not in use. There is nothing greater than light to influence our sense of well-being. This is true of seasons, of gardens, and of any interior, in terms of day and night. Too many interiors are over-lit by sunlight on glass. Mediterranean people learned eons ago to put shutters over their windows so that they would not become heat convectors. For the same reason, the Japanese roof over their windowed walls—this is something I did at LongHouse. With building the house came great costs but considerable savings, particularly gifts from manufacturers to this iconic project, including both floor tiles and fireproof roof tiles. The stucco walls inside and out were cost-effective and will never need painting. Those inside are "Japanese plaster" mixed with clay and rice straw to resist soil and blemishes.

OPPOSITE In a living room–sitting area are grouped a 1927 tea table by the Swedish furniture designer Bruno Mathsson, and with antique Thai baskets. The chairs are by the British-born designer T.H. Robsjohn-Gibbings, the daybed is from Larsen Furniture, the butterfly stool is by Sori Yanagi, and the tall lacquered Chinese chest dates from about 1900. The rug is Japanese rattan.

OVERLEAF The living room and veranda have 25-foot-high pitched ceilings, while the airy stair atrium reaches a height of 38 feet. So does its west window wall, screened from the sun by broad-bladed shutters. This great height was indeed scary until the double staircase floated through it.

LEFT The passageway between the living room and the foyer is marked with Wharton Esherick's carved chestnut archway from the Curtis Bok house in Radnor, Pennsylvania, dating from 1933. More important than cost savings have been the increased amenities in this highly personal house, such as the blocking out and reception of sunlight, the variety of ceiling heights, and the placement of windows where the views are at their prime best. I'm not advocating skimping, nor doing without, but exchanging economy for something more meaningful. In other words, a subsidy—even better when exchanging a problem for a plus. Look for these possibilities! They reduce costs considerably.

The two tall conservatories are roofed with a double layer of bronze-tinted glass (with three inches of air between them) to become the most pleasant place to be. Plants love this, but so do people. Sunlight: Keeping out, letting in. Six-foot-deep eaves wholly protect windows from solar heat. The south-facing wall is even more protected. The veranda with a 16-foot-wide roof above not only sheds rain, but also shields people from solar heat. If glare and solar heat are not desirable, light is, entering LongHouse through a 65-foot-long tinted skylight at the axis of the ceiling high above. (On the third level, this is often screened by a horizontal baffle of reflective solar cloth.) Most of the electric lighting at LongHouse emanates from either inexpensive floor cans or torchières lighting the ceilings. Dimmers not only afford optimum light levels but lower electric costs. To be in sunlight when it is freezing outdoors is especially conducive to friendship. Curiously, glazed roofs are rare—even though their cost is not prohibitive and the heat-gain/loss is no more than with heavily insulated roofs.

OPPOSITE The west side of the living room shows deep window seats and massive shutters. The tall woodcut is by American sculptor and print maker Leonard Baskin.

LEFT The 24-foot-long peaked, ceilinged breezeway floats above the guest terrace below, to connect with the minor wing beyond. Windows on both sides provide views east and west as well as copious daylight. This space is unheated except for a small Danish fireplace providing welcome warmth. Furnishings change with the season. The summer seating shown here is from Larsen Furniture. The carpet is rattan.

OPPOSITE Raising the principal floor—and its open veranda—welcomes cooling breezes and improved views. (The Hamptons have no hills.)

RIGHT In one corner of the expansive veranda overlooking the lotus pond, guests can be accommodated at two different-sized tables. Often one is in shade, the other in sun, but both profit from the fresh breezes and spectacular views.

LEFT The west façade is flanked by a long tiled walk, skirted by a wide band of the low-growing plants of the Scree Garden and backed by a tall hemlock hedge. The flat Scree Garden is named for its similarity to the gravelly scree disclosed by melting glaciers. The soil is thin and the drainage is good, with full sun for an informal range of close-to-ground plants including wildflowers, sedums, and many bulbs, and, from February, a variety of iris, anemones, and species tulips. The low fertility ensures little change from year to year, but an eye-pleasing panorama over seasons. Beyond are the lawns and landscaping that are enchantingly visible from the raised main floor of the house. Japanese sculptor Takashi Soga's steel tower is kinetic, as the column under the boulder shifts slowly in the wind.

RIGHT While most American homes are encircled by foundation plantings surrounded by lawns, LongHouse is not. Instead, the house rests on a wide platform of coarse gravel. This platform feeds the French drain tiles that carry rainwater to the pond.

LEFT The 50-foot-long and seven-foot-wide lap pool was originally designed to run down the center of the summer living room. When I decided that, without sunlight, the water would remain too cold, Charles Forberg, the architect, moved it to the center of the West Wing, forming a cross-axis to the house. The pool now has increasingly wider patios on either side, to form an area in which to socialize.

RIGHT A gurgling fountain spills into the narrow rill, recycling water to the lap pool. On either side, Dennis Schrader of Landcraft Environments planted tropical borders that bloom from May until frost. That the pool is painted black and is only a meter deep induces quick warming.

THE GARDEN

Buying plants small and early is key. The hemlock hedges planted along former field boundaries were muddied in, bare root, for ten cents each! Small trees are quite affordable, especially when they are on sale. And, of course, we received many plants as gifts. Most people start gardens with a master plan and budget, but I, instead, recall the Chinese proverb, "Be an open bowl that some opportunity may fall in" to welcome gifts, opportunities, and transplants—or what's on hand to expand over time. Dunes require very little maintenance: No irrigation, fertilizing, or mowing. Large lawns and ground-cover areas are easily maintained, as are graveled areas and the evergreens. Low-cost bamboo stands require no maintenance other than removing dead canes for garden stakes. The common fear of "running bamboo" (most bamboo in temperate zones does take over) is easily resolved by planting in a sturdy blanket. The combination of near and distant views becomes even more satisfying when each enhances the other—especially beautiful in the "borrowed scenery" of Japanese gardens, with their veiled views of adjoining areas. Seasonal changes multiply these pleasures. The fact that LongHouse is a four-season garden was learned in Japan on my many winter visits, when form and texture dominate the landscape. Blossoms seemed too ephemeral—especially to this weekender.

OPPOSITE When we were given 30 tall fastigiate hornbeam trees, landscape architect Peter Hornbeck arranged them so as to create a second cross-axis. This arrangement became unique when he laid out a progression of one, two, three, four, and five pairs of trees. This elongation took no more time or effort than conventional rows, but created a much longer allée, and is much more dynamic. Now that these tall, sheared trees are mature, the tension between their uniformity, in contrast to shaggy natural foliage, is very pleasing. The stone piece is by the Japanese sculptor Izumi Masatoshi, who works in Mure, Japan. This work, shown in the sculpture court, feels both substantial and inevitable.

RIGHT To us, it seems amazing that there are so few such ponds, as they are the easiest and least costly feature to build. A pond also remains lowest to maintain. Peter's Pond is a favorite place for all seasons. In winter, ice supports a field of snow, then disappears with the remaining vegetation. By spring, the open expanse of water becomes a mirror for bursts of cherry blossoms and the earliest daffodils. Come summer, we enjoy a thousand water lilies, followed by tall, exotic lotus. The frogs, fish, and birds entertain us, and the swallows gobble the mosquitoes.

LEFT When I was eight years old, I watched a neighbor split granite slabs for a substantial fountain. Now, at the edge of Peter's Pond, this fountain is the focus from both the plaza and the veranda that overlooks it. Watching birds bathe in it is a pleasant diversion. Beyond is the ever-changing panorama of Peter's Pond.

RIGHT Although the gardens are still wintry in late March, crowds of daffodils sing out cheerfully. Planted over four decades in a hundred varieties, they have multiplied many times over. As these bulbs are poisonous, they are not eaten by deer and other animals. Frothy, hay-scented ferns will soon spring up, masking the bulbs' browning foliage.

LEFT In May, four Korean cherry trees explode into clouds of heavy blossoms. Andrée Putman, the French designer and a close friend, designed the highback bench that invites relaxation beside the mirror-like pond.

RIGHT A prime feature of the large Pink Garden is a block-long rose arbor created by using low-cost, durable supports that are a cluster of 30 foot-long rebars from a stone quarry. Bamboo poles now form the lateral supports, to allow pink climbing roses to extend their blooms, while pink clematis montana plays a supporting role with the lush greenery, including the banks of geranium. Curved walkways, which do not reveal their destinations, are favored here.
With increased traffic, gravel of various colors has replaced many of our former grass paths.

LEFT When a Reserve office was built, instead of carting away the foundation soil, we leveled the otherwise sloping area of the garden and created the Squash Court, completing it for SquashFest, when hundreds of school children were given heirloom squash seeds to grow over the summer to compete for the best, largest, and most unusual squash.
They were given ribbons at the SquashFest party in the Fall, when we sculpted squash, printed with it, made music with dried squash, and ate it in new ways. We built tiers of stone boxes to ceremoniously display rare squash plants. Both the blue stone slabs and gravel were recycled.

RIGHT Raised just a foot above the Squash Court, the Lear Pavilion has been recently painted red to be more inviting. Weatherproof Sunbrella® cushions welcome visitors. The turquoise pots are vintage Thai rain jars.

SCULPTURE

Sculpture is best experienced outdoors in full highlight and shadow, its solidity contrasting with airy foliage. Sculpture in the garden forms strong focal points, sometimes anchoring vistas. At LongHouse, this is also our principal means of change, as works on loan are often here for only a year or two. Both artists and galleries are quite willing to lend work not on exhibit, because art storage is costly and so overcrowded that the work cannot be viewed. LongHouse is also an ideal showcase. Strategic sculpture placement encourages non-gardeners to tour the garden. We try to have sculpture from a broad range of media, scale, and subject. Large ceramics—old and new—are in evidence, as are kinetic works.

OPPOSITE *Spheres*, by New York installation artist Grace Knowlton, are built of cement over meshed wire armatures, and have been in the LongHouse collection for over 30 years.

LEFT East Hampton-based artist Eric Fischl's bronze 2002 *Tumbling Woman* is a memorial to the victims of 9/11.

OPPOSITE The two 1998 works by American sculptor Lynda Benglis have human forms. The artist calls them "pedmarks," rather than using the words "hand-prints" or "footprints"— *Migrating Pedmarks*, a bronze with a black-and-white patina in the foreground and *Cloak-Wave Pedmarks*, a bronze with a black patina and polished bronze interior in the background—recall Japanese kimonos. Benglis wants to draw attention to the similarities between human and animal life, creating pieces that might appear to have been made in the past by a prehistoric monster.

RIGHT Perhaps because of Dale Chihuly's understanding of both glass and water as being translucent, he has often combined the two, as in the 2006 installation *Blue and Purple Boat.* Several versions have been exhibited here. The boats are, of course, just large containers for his assembled work. Many of these are raucously polychrome, but this one gains from repeated "reeds" of cobalt.

LEFT Chihuly's *Cobalt Spears*, from around 1995, remain at LongHouse from the second showing of his work in the garden. Their luminosity derives from a repeated dipping in clear glass, then in cobalt. Anchored to the ground on stainless steel rods topped with rubber balls, they survive any kind of weather. Installed each year in a different garden, they remain our most popular exhibit. As Dale Chihuly has never forgotten that I pushed him in 1964 to study glass blowing with Harvey Littleton, we have been friends for 50 years. The LongHouse collection of his work includes all periods, and his first two exhibitions of glass in a garden were held here.

RIGHT American artist Sol LeWitt's tall sculpture was sited through the process of digital imagery to determine both its location and placement. Now the changes of sunlight and seasons enhance its rich surfaces, and raked pine needles become the resilient floor around it. Perhaps because they can perceive the material and structure of the Sol LeWitt, children are enamored with it as "a magical city." Today, this artist is best known for his gigantic wall paintings, usually crisp geometry achieved with taped edges. But in his lifetime he was thought of as a sculptor of unique media. This, his last piece, was made when he was terminally ill, and we are proud to have it. The place was created for it, and it was conceived for the space, each aspect calculated by its numbered blocks. The only part not seen is the substantial base of poured cement.

RIGHT When I was told that the lowest lay of land would not have enough runoff for a pond, I recalled flying over the handsome, grassed-over Celtic ringforts of Ireland. I realized that using subsoil from digging a basement at Round House, we could build an amphitheater for performances. After a great deal of shaping with hand rakes, then plugging the surface with Japanese zoysia grass that wouldn't need mowing, weeding or watering, it worked! The amphitheater is the setting for the tall *NAWA Axis for Peace* by the Kyoto-based Japanese sculptor Mariyo Yagi. Its durable, non-fading textile was made by Sunbrella®. The ten bronze sculptures circling the amphitheater are cast from stoneware by American artist of Greek descent, Peter Voulkos.

LEFT The 25 cast bronze *Warriors* by Chinese artist Yue Minjun, have been installed in many configurations at LongHouse, including this marching order.

RIGHT Formerly a croquet lawn, de Kooning Place, is the flattest area of the garden. With its access for caterers from the service yard next door, it is a fine setting for large events. The breadth of a weeping Blue Atlas Cedar is the perfect backdrop for American artist Willem de Kooning's 1969–1982 *Reclining Figure*, installed in 2005. The sculpture was lowered over the cedar by a giant crane without crossing the lawns—a small miracle. The "snow" on top of the cedar—actually a volunteer clematis vine—reflects the white Hydrangea tardiva.

OPPOSITE While many of New York's sculptural gardens favor abstraction, we welcome figurative work—including the 2002 *Legacy Mantle (Mao's Jacket)* by Chinese artist Sui Jianguo. The heavy iron from which it is made evokes and reinforces the unswervingly dictatorial subject.

LEFT Potter Shin Sang Ho of Korea favors animals as subjects, in all sizes, for indoors and outside. From his one-man show here, a herd of young rams, *Dream of Africa*, elicits smiles. In white glazed stoneware, they are as playful as young kids.

LEFT Japanese sculptor Takashi Soga's bronze sheet, painted steel, 2007, *Eye of the Ring*, kinetic sculpture echoes the ten-foot voids of Buckminster Fuller's 1965 *Fly's Eye Dome* that can be seen behind it. The fact that Soga's upper ring floats with the slightest breeze seems miraculous. Framed views through the open rounds of both sculptures are amazing. A propitious snowfall reduced the whole scene to black and white.

RIGHT Veiled views become a double pleasure, such as the look of American architect Buckminster Fuller's *Fly's Eye Dome* through a copse of tall Korean bamboo. The veiling is multiplied because, in addition, our eye pierces through the dome walls.

EPILOGUE:
ON COLLECTING

Historically, princes, or at least merchant princes, were the collectors. Today there is reason for all of us to collect. Building collections of any size or material is the surest means to affirming our identity and a powerful hedge against being only a statistic. With both government and industry wanting us to be as predictable as sheep—and tongue-tied and butterfingered to boot—our primary need is to reinforce our personal identities. Collecting—the owning of a unique body of objects—is probably not as vital as sharing enthusiasm for what has special meaning for us, which reminds us of the existence of excellence or offers us insights. This can be a work of art that is also functional—such as "wares" for entertaining. Wharton Esherick, the greatest furniture maker of the 20th century, had been a friend since 1952. At LongHouse, we have the finest collection of Esherick works in a private collection.

OPPOSITE Displaying a collection need not be a precious or costly undertaking. These ethnographic baskets are simply hanging on a wooden wall. The ones with dark and light patterns suggest that basketry, among man's first tools, was the forerunner of weaving.

A collection can be anything—and can be made of expensive objects or not. I recall an impoverished Polish weaver's walls emblazoned with exotic pressed leaves—a great effect at no cost. My own collecting started when I was three years old, and was of seedling trees gathered in the woods. Perhaps what I am trying to say is that collecting relates to the drive for territory, an instinct possibly stronger than life itself. Of course, territorial drive connotes a sense of place. My grandfathers, who carved their farms out of raw prairie, felt that the whole village was home, and 'theirs.' Today, most of us control only a small, indifferent space and therefore have the need to make it personal so that we can feel "these digs are mine!" For me, collections that enhance one's personal environment seem more meaningful than coins or stamps. Much as I love seeing what is ancient or remote, the objects of our time bring me more pleasure, and I have not made acquisitions unless I expect to share them with friends. The phrase I believe suits this best is "furnishings and craft." Both denote broad universes—functional or not—in a great swath of media, with something to suit every taste and budget. The unusual is provocative, with its cost or "value" not as important as how innovative it is. For example, one of our most successful buffets had all the dishes served on fresh banana leaves!

OPPOSITE One bay of the covered shelves in the dining room shows off a broad array of modern craft conveyed in black and white. Most are by American potters. The black and white box on the upper left is a double cloth by American fiber artist Kay Sekimachi.

OVERLEAF Three favorite potters who work with porcelain in the LongHouse collection, include Turkish artist Alev Siesbye's coiled piece on a minimal base, *left*, two filigree forms by the British potter Ursula Morley Price, *center*, and carved porcelain discs by the American-born Marc Leuthold, *right*. Hanging above is a 1983 pencil drawing of the Siena Cathedral by George Kozmon.

RIGHT In the dining room, the red bench by Wharton Esherick was originally made for a porch, which explains the infrequency of the use of softwood and the fact that it has been painted.

OVERLEAF The repeated forms of the late American potter Richard De Vere have in common their ultra-matte glazes, achieved through the artist's technique of multiple firings.

ARTWORKS
PAGE 1 Gaston Lachaise, *Standing Woman*, 1932, bronze, 88¼ in. × 44¾ in. × 25⅜ in. Collection The Lachaise Foundation, ©2016 The Lachaise Foundation
PAGE 2–3, 121 Kiki Smith, *Women with Sheep (Three Women, Three Sheep)*, 2009, bronze, overall installation dimensions variable, courtesy of the Artist and Pace Gallery, page 121 (detail)
PAGE 6 Yoko Ono, *Play It By Trust*, 1999, marble dust, concrete, 36 in. x 198 in. x 198 in. Permanent Loan, courtesy of the artist, 2008. ©2016 Yoko Ono
PAGE 12 Judith Shea, *Idol*, 2011–12, bronze, stainless steel, aluminum, cast, 77 in. x 36 in. x 36 in. Collection of the artist
PAGE 14 Wharton Esherick, dining table, 1939, MCMXXV, walnut, rawhide, phenol, 72 in. x 31 in. x 28 in. Collection Longhouse Reserve, gift of Jack Larsen, 2013
PAGE 26 Toshiko Takaezu, *Almost Closed Form*, c.1962, stoneware, hand-built, 27½ in. x 26 in. x 22 in. Larsen Collection, promised gift to the LongHouse Heserve
PAGE 35 Magdalena Abakanowicz, *Rabdomante (Black Standing Figure)*, 1999, aluminum, cast, 66½ in. x 25 in. x 34 in. Private Collection, courtesy of the Marlborough Gallery, NY
PAGE 45, 95 Dale Chihuly, *Cobalt Reeds*, 2000, glass, dimensions variable from 50 to 96 in. high, LHR Collection, gift of the artist, 2003
PAGE 56: Wharton Esherick, Archway for Curtis Bok house, from passageway between dining room and foyer, Radnor, PA, c.1933, carved chestnut, 102 in. x 91 in. x 17 in. Collection Longhouse Reserve, gift of Jack Larsen, 2013
PAGE 65 Takashi Soga, *Floating Rain*, 2000, painted steel, stone, 129 in. x 76 in. x 22 in. Collection LongHouse Reserve, purchase, Acquisition Fund, 2002
PAGE 70 Judy Kensley McKie, *Elephant Bench*, 2008, Bardiglio marble, 2/6, 17½ in. x 70 in. x 25½ in. Longhouse Reserve Collection, partial gift by the artist and Pritam & Eames, with the generous support of the following donors: Elizabeth and Ted Rogers, Lauren Bedell and Michael Mills, Barbara Slifka, Katja Goldman and Michael Sonnenfeldt, Jack Lenor Larsen, Jim Zajac
PAGE 72 Izumi Masatoshi, *Fuyu*, 2008, Swedish granite, steel, stone, 59 in. x 59 in. x 33 in. Collection of the artist, courtesy of Japonesque Gallery, San Francisco, CA
PAGE 79 Atsuya Tominaga, *Ninguen*, 2008, marble, various dimensions. Collection of LongHouse Reserve. Gift of the artist and Ippodo Gallery, 2012
PAGE 88 Grace Knowlton, *Untitled (5 Round Forms)*, 1985, steel, meshed wire, concrete, styrofoam, assembled; dimensions variable. Larsen Collection, promised gift to LongHouse Reserve
PAGE 90 Eric Fischl, *Tumbling Woman*, 2002, bronze, cast, 37 in. x 74 in. x 50 in. Collection of the artist
PAGE 91 *Migrating Pedmarks*, 1998, bronze with black-and-white patina, 87 in. x 135 in. x 96 in. Courtesy the artist and Cheim & Read, New York. *Cloak-Wave Pedmarks*, 1998, bronze with black patina and polished bronze interior, 85½ in. x 86 in. x 56 in. Courtesy the artist and Cheim & Read, New York
PAGES 92–93 Dale Chihuly, *Blue and Purple Boat*, 2006, blown glass, 72 in. x 216 in. x 84 in. Collection of the artist
PAGE 96–97 Sol LeWitt, *Irregular Progression, High #7*, 2006, concrete, blocks, 252 in. x 80 in. x 192 in. Permanent Loan, courtesy of Pace

CAPTIONS ENDPAPERS New York based Roberto Dutesco photographed Jack Lenor Larsen strolling up and down Ray's Way. BACK OF FRONT ENDPAPER AND PAGE 1 Designed by Jack Lenor Larsen, the *Black Mirror* is a water feature that was installed by Ray Smith and Associates. The bronze sculpture, *Standing Woman*, 1932, is by the French-born artist Gaston Lachaise. PAGES 2–3 A pastoral scene of bronzes, the 2009 *Women with Sheep*, by Kiki Smith, has been set on a bed of Pachysandra under the beech trees, and along a path that leads visitors to the Black Mirror. "Elegance usually results from subtraction" is a mantra at LongHouse. When the tall, scraggly hornbeam hedge became infested, we spent a long time considering how to replace it. But when the diseased plants were removed, a stupendous view appeared. It is now our favorite vista. Many of us think one more thing would be wonderful! Try removal instead. BACK OF BACK ENDPAPERS A detail of Kiki Smith's *Women with Sheep* is part of the artist's installation.

PHOTOGRAPHY CREDITS Roberto Dutesco: Front endpapers, 6, 14, 59, back endpapers. Ingalls Photography: Back of front endpapers-1, 4, 8, 34-35, 50, 52, 55, 91, 114-115, 118. Dell Cullum: 2-3, 10-11. Robert Grant: 16, 18-19, 24. Herbert Migdoll: 20. Phillip Ennis: 22-23, 25. Matko Tomicic: 26-29, 38-39, 51, 62, 72, 84-85, 88, 90, 92-93, 96-101, 104-107, back of back endpapers. Molly Chappellet: 30-31. Joanne Sohn: 40-49, 64-65, 68-71, 76-83, 86-87, 94-95, 102-103, 108-109. Eric Laignel: 54, 56-57, 60-61, 74-75, 116-117. Peter Olsen: 63. Paul Ryan/Juliana Balint: 110. David Frazier: 113.
All Larsen Design Studio textile designs are owned by Cowtan & Tout, Inc. www.cowtan.com.

Wildenstein, with support of Barbara Slifka, M.O.E. Masonry,
© 2016 The LeWitt Estate/Artist Rights Society (ARS), New York
PAGE 98 Peter Voulkos, *Alegria*, 1994-2000, bronze, from clay models,
50 in. x 28 in. Courtesy of Mussi Family Trust/Chaco Gallery
PAGE 99 Mariyo Yagi, *NAWA Axis for Peace*, 2014, Sunbrella® fabric,
sewing, stuffing, twisting; 396 in. x 48 in. x 48 in. Collection of the artist
Peter Voulkos, *Chaco*, 1994-2000, bronze, from clay models,
56 in. x 28 in. x 28 in. Courtesy of Mussi Family Trust/Chaco Gallery
PAGES 100–101 Yue Minjun, *Chinese Contemporary Warriors*, 2005,
bronze, cast, 71¾ in. x 21¾ in. x 21¾ in. Private Collection
PAGES 102-103 Willem de Kooning, *Reclining Figure*, 1969-1982,
bronze, 67 in. x 130 in. x 96 in. Collection The Willem de Kooning
Foundation, ©2016 The Willem de Kooning Foundation/Artist Rights
Society (ARS), New York
PAGE 104 Sui Jianguo, *Legacy Mantle (Mao Jacket)*, 2002, cast iron,
117 ⅝ in. x 97 ³⁄₁₆ in. x 57 ⅝ in. Collection of Larry Warsh
Page 105 Shin Sang-Ho, *Dream of Africa* (small totems), 2004, ceramic,
hand-built, glazed, various dimensions. Private collection
Pages 106-107 Buckminster Fuller, *Fly's Eye Dome*, 1997, fiberglass,
336 in. x 396 in. x 396 in. Designed by Buckminster Fuller and produced
by John Kuhtik, 1997. Collection John Kuhtik
Takashi Soga, *Sea of the Ear Rings*, 2005, painted steel,
168 in. x 168 in. x 168 in. Collection of the artist
Pages 116–117 Wharton Esherick, Bench (painted pine), 1959, pine,
painted; 16¾ in. x 85⅝ in. x 31 in. Collection LongHouse Reserve,
purchase, Larsen Fund, 1996
Gregory Roberts, *Kala Pani (Blackwater)*, 1996, carved honeycomb
ceramic, 26½ in. x 15 in. x 15 in. Collection LongHouse Reserve
Acquisition Fund purchase, 1996

BIBLIOGRAPHY

Azalea Stuart Thorpe and Jack Larsen, *Elements of Weaving*,
Doubleday & Co., 1967
Jack Lenor Larsen with Dr. Alfred Buhler and Bronwen and Garrett
Solyom, *The Dyer's Art: Ikat, Batik, Plangi*, Van Nostrand Reinhold, 1971
Mildred Constantine and Jack Lenor Larsen, *Beyond Craft: The Art
Fabric*, Van Nostrand Reinhold, 1972
Jack Lenor Larsen with Jeanne Weeks, *Fabric for Interiors*,
Van Nostrand Reinhold, 1975
Jack Lenor Larsen with Mildred Constantine, *The Art Fabric:
Mainstream*, Van Nostrand Reinhold, 1981
Jack Lenor Larsen with Betty Freudenheim, *Interlacing:
The Elemental Fabric*, Kodansha International, 1986
Jack Lenor Larsen, *Material Wealth: Living with Luxurious Fabrics*,
Abbeville Press Inc., Thames & Hudson, 1989
Jack Lenor Larsen, *The Tactile Vessel: New Basket Forms*, Erie Art
Museum, PA, 1989
Jack Lenor Larsen, *A Weaver's Memoir*, Harry N. Abrams, Inc.,
New York, NY, 1998
David McFadden, Lotus Stack, Mildred Friedman, *Jack Lenor Larsen:
Creator & Collector,* exhibition catalog, Merrell Publishers, 2004
Molly Chappellet, *Jack Lenor Larsen's LongHouse*,
Chronicle Books, 2010

DEDICATION

I dedicate this book to those mentors who encouraged me to push beyond the normal into special, far-flung interests—mine! These include some special teachers, scout leaders, and friends. Better yet, when I was both a bohemian and postgraduate, the mentors were often a generation older, lending encouragement or helping hands or sometimes, a commission. Attracted to those who knew more and traveled farther, I was welcome to join in. Soon, a weaver making cloths for these designers and architects seemed like getting their approval, and, if nothing else, certainly a financial subsidy. Because of them, I didn't need a job, but played long and hard. I also taught others to follow their hearts. If I am proud of protégés like Dale Chihuly and many less known than he, my favorite mentor is Charles Forberg, the architect with whom I shared the design of three airlines, a dozen showrooms and exhibitions, and three personal houses. He accepted my norm of designing as we went along, and our working as Craft Makers. I mention him because I am still learning from his skills in ordering sturdy materials at LongHouse. This is a deep pleasure I enjoy sharing.

ACKNOWLEDGMENTS

For this, my twelfth book, conceived of slowly while writing another on people I have known, I thank many. My personal assistant, Crystal Cooper, and the LongHouse staff come first, plus past editors who taught me much, and the patience of friend Peter Olsen. The artists we have exhibited at LongHouse and the photographers are key. So are the great gardens inspiring this landscape and those, like Ray Smith, who shape it still. The LongHouse Board and committee members have for decades encouraged this evolving Case Study. Lastly, I'm grateful for the wisdom, the encouragement, and the taste of Suzanne Slesin, Frederico Farina, and Kelly Koester of Pointed Leaf Press, who have shaped this book. —JACK LENOR LARSEN, EAST HAMPTON, APRIL 2016

Learning from LongHouse and the LongHouse movie are made possible by generous contributions from Dorothy Lichtenstein, John Lawrence Githens, Sandy and Steve Perlbinder, Barbara Slifka, Neda Young, Linda Usher and Malcolm Lambe, Toni Ross, Susan and Richard Marcus, Ginger and Marlin Miller, Elizabeth and Mark Levine, Anne and Charles Roos, Bruce Sloane, Nina Gillman, and Sandra and Louis Grotta.

Publisher/Editorial Director **SUZANNE SLESIN**

Creative Director **FREDERICO FARINA**

PRINTED AND BOUND IN ITALY FIRST EDITION 10 9 8 7 6 5 4 3 2 1 ISBN: 978-1-938461-34-7 Library of Congress Control Number: 2016936351